Adona ~

Thank

The Lord bless you !

Make Warm Noises

Make Warm Noises

Gloria Gaither

Photos by Bill Grine

impact
books
Nashville, Tennessee

Contents

to bill

. . . And so because
you walked an aisle
into my life some
ninety-six short months
ago, I add to the
coffer of my treasure
    one
           more
                year.

You've filled that
treasure chest I
call my life with
other beauties too —
    a dancing nymph;
a cheery, chubby cherub;
    and now
a wise and gentle prince.
    You have
painted our walls
    with sunshine
and helped us fill
the spaces in between
them with joy and
    laughter.

You have taught me
the meaning of delight
and made me beautiful
because you say I am!
You have given me the

      courage
to love as I dreamed
so long that I could —
not only in response
to a lover, but in
      response to *life*.

      Thank you . . .

for making me what
      I have become.

It isn't that I'm
      much at all —
It's only that
      I wear your love so well.

PART I

"UNLESS YE BECOME AS LITTLE CHILDREN..."

Thank God for Children

No one would dispute the fact that children say the cutest things! Many otherwise awkward moments have been made pleasant, many impossible barriers spanned by the sharing of stories about little sons and daughters, nieces and nephews, and "darling" grandchildren. But children are more than cute, and their commentary on life is much more than accidentally apropos.

Children possess an uncanny ability to cut to the core of the issue, expose life to the bone, and strip away the barnacles that cling to the hull of our too-sophisticated pseudo-civilization. One reason for this, I believe, is that children have not mastered our fine art of deception we call "finesse." Another is that they are so "lately come from God" that faith and trust are second nature to them. They have not acquired the obstructions to faith that come with education; they possess instead unrefined wisdom, a gift from God.

Jesus himself prayed, "I thank thee, O Father, Lord of heaven and earth, because thou hast hid these things from the wise and prudent and revealed them unto babes." (Matt. 11:25) I thank God that our home has been blessed with children who allow us to glimpse the Divine and teach us to comprehend the profound!

Page from a Mother's Diary

Today when I look at our new baby bed, waiting for its tiny occupant, I am torn between a physical desire to have our child arrive and an emotional fear of the responsibility that will come with that little life. Women who look forward to having a baby with never a fear must be overgrown little girls expecting a new doll that not only says "ma-ma" but is really alive. I keep thinking of the many times as a four or five-year-old that I held my doll in my arms and prayed with all my might that it would come to life. I would watch its little eyelashes so closely and then when nothing happened, I would wonder if God were there at all. I probably came as close to being an atheist at those times as I ever did in my life. But how very much like the doubters so verbal in our time I was! My faith was clouded by ignorance and short-sightedness. What if God had granted my request and given me charge of a soul at a time when my own was a mere hesitant bud?

Our adult requests must be like that at times: the prayers we pray for God to spare the life of a loved one, the times we ask that some problem be worked out in our way. If only we could see through the eyes of God!

But now in a few short weeks I am to look into another little face in my arms, and this time, as I watch the little eyelashes flicker and the little mouth move, my prayer will be different, and I hope, wiser. "Oh, God, You have given me a vacant soul, an untaught conscience, a life of clay. Put

14

your big hands around mine and guide my hands as a teacher guides the childish fingers that hold their first crayon, so that every time I make a mark on this life, it will be your mark. When my hands mold this clay, may the impressions be, in reality, made by the movement of your hands and directed by your perfect thoughts."

Make
Warm Noises

"Just let me play in my room all by myself! But could you stay up here and work? I want to be by myself, but Mommy, make warm noises I can hear."

Independence and security — solitude, but not loneliness — to be alone, together. A child expresses at three what we all feel all through our lives: the struggle to be on our own while still securely bolstered by those who really love us, the need sometimes to be alone in order to work, to create, to think and to express ourselves, yet not engulfed by loneliness. Sometimes we are not guileless or honest enough to say it, but a child is. Mommy, leave me alone, but don't go away. Always be there. Stay within earshot. Let me hear you making the familiar, happy sounds of the day. Mommy, stay near — and make warm noises.

An honest relationship with God is like that. He always allows us to the freedom to think, to create, even to question and doubt; He gives us the gentle assurance and secure love we need to develop the best in our independent spirit. But He is always near to guide, to whisper, to work, to make a way. And if we ever develop the best in ourselves, we need the power that comes from being certain that God is there, so sure of His love that we can work on in confidence at the task before us, the heart praying in simple faith, "Stay near me, Lord Jesus — I cannot be free to live, if I cannot hear *You*."

The "Pass"

Suzanne's pacifier presented a major dilemma for all of us. While Bill and I debated the pro's and con's of removing it from existence, Suzanne went happily about with it firmly implanted in its accustomed position and gave not one thought to the possible psychological implications.

She reached her second birthday and still no sign of the "giving it up" stage other parents so glibly talked about. We began to worry. One of these days, we thought, she would start dating and at the rate she was going she would still have that thing. That was Bill's verdict. So we decided to take it away from her there and then.

We thought we had problems before; we really had problems after that. She had been such an articulate child up until that time, but within a week she was stuttering pitiably. She had problems with her training habits and suffered relapses into babyhood. We were at our wits' end.

I read Dr. Spock. Bill talked to our minister who had done research on stuttering in the two-year-old. We both asked advice from our doctor. We decided to give back the pacifier — and was she a happy soul!

When some problem confronted her she simply said, "Give me my pass," and she would go into a corner someplace. The "pass" seemed to be enough to relieve her fears and anxieties. Her habits returned to normal in no time. The symptoms were not there but the "pass" problem was still with us.

This went on for quite some time. Finally, one day all on her own, she came up to me with the "pass" in her hand and said, "Here Mommy, take this thing; it's empty!" She had discovered that there was nothing in it anymore, that it was just a pacifier, a crutch, a phony.

How often we adults limp through life with one crutch or another. Sometimes the pacifiers seem to suffice, and we get by and even trick ourselves into thinking we are happy and fulfilled. But someday if we are to find out what real life is all about, we must go in childlike honesty to the Heavenly Father and say, "Here Father, take it all — the sham, the pretense, the facade; it's empty! I have spent my life majoring in minors. I have been so busy making a living I have failed to make a life. Give me, now, the courage to face life head-on. Fill me with the real thing."

Turn the Church On!

Not long ago Bill and I were to be in a certain church for an evening of gospel music. We arrived in town early, just as the shades of winter's nightfall were creeping along North Carolina's hills. We went straight to the church to make necessary arrangements for the program and found that although the building was unlocked, we had arrived ahead of the pastor and janitor. The church was dark and the heat had not yet been turned up. Our three-year-old daughter ran ahead of us, as she always does, in search of the sanctuary. Flinging the double swinging doors wide open, she rushed a few steps into the dark auditorium, stopped, wrapped her little arms around herself, then called at the top of her voice, "Daddy! Turn the church on!"

The church of today has more facilities with which to work than at any other time in history. We have better buildings, more varied avenues of service, the fantastic tools of mass communication, the power of united effort with other churches. Yet with all this, there must be the warmth of the personal touch, the undercurrent of sincere concern, the gentleness of genuine love. Those who come to us must find not only the fixtures, but the "Presence." Behind the strong, oaken doors of the church the needy must find a real strength that can make a difference in their lives. If the church is to be a tool that God can use in this century, it is we who have met Him face to face that must "turn the church on."

O Father of compassion, help me to care more!

Make me an expression on earth of God's power and light. May I be the warmth and the shine. Help me to throw the switches I can reach to "turn the church on"!

Woolly Worms
and Stuff Like That

She had always been a stranger to fear. Woolly worms, garden snakes, night crawlers, and three-inch praying mantises were all her friends. Climbing trees, spinning around monkey bars, jumping from any height or diving to any depth held no threat for her.

I remember one time when her grandma retrieved her from a three-story spiral staircase in Stephen Foster's "Ole Kentucky Home" just as she was about to jump from the top, thoroughly convinced that by flapping her arms, she could fly as she had watched the robins do in the garden.

So it was nothing new when at a church in Wichita one night she turned a somersault over a stair banister without counting the cost and whopped her head on a brick step, a trick that left a goose-egg on her lower skull, half big enough to put her hat on. Like any worried mother I checked her eyes for signs of concussion, put an ice pack on the knot and gave her a lecture on the *dangers* in life, one being bad bumps that could cause brain damage to a healthy four-year-old.

The next morning in the motel, she woke up to find the bump greatly diminished. "Well, Mother," she bubbled, "your kid survived!" Then she snuggled up beside me and softly added, "I know why . . . I heard you praying for me."

So often I have worried about the bigger dangers and traps life places in the path of our little ones. How can we be sure that our children will survive the encounters with evil, steer clear of filth and not be spiritually maimed for life by silly miscalculations and foolish involvements. It has always seemed to me a gross mistake that young people have to make the most important of life's choices during their turbulent youth when, emotionally and spiritually, they are least fitted with wisdom and maturity. How, then?

"But I have prayed for thee. . . ." AND I BELIEVE!

Sizing Up Values

As soon as she was old enough to put a penny in a slot she would always spot the gum ball machines as soon as one was anywhere in sight and ask for a penny. One time, though, she tried to put a penny in a prize machine that could use only nickels. I caught her in time, explained that the prize inside was more valuable than a piece of gum, and that she'd need a more valuable coin.

Several weeks later she was sitting in church holding tightly in her fist the quarter we had given her for the offering. I noticed that when the usher came to our row it was taking her longer than usual to get her money into the plate. She was looking intently at the coins and bills which were already there. After we had put in our contributions and the plate had passed on, she lifted her serious little face and whispered, "Mother! We don't give pennies for Jesus. He's worth more than that, isn't he?" "Yes, He is," I answered.

In the ensuing silence I remembered how often I had heard it said that our actions teach more than our words, and I thought of how often I had lost sight of that. I kept shuddering to think what I would have taught my daughter about God if I had absent-mindedly handed her a penny. . . .

"I Love You Thirty-Seven"

When we first brought the new baby home from the hospital, she was so helpless. It seemed that every cog in the works of our household revolved around her.

But how we loved her! At last, after all the months of waiting and guessing, here was a tangible bundle of innocent humanity that we could love. But that love went all one way. She soaked it up like a thirsty sponge and did not learn for a long time that love is to be given as well as received.

For months she was here only to be cared for, fed, washed, and made comfortable. What a thrill it was when one day she timidly lifted her chubby little hand and gently patted my cheek! Her first real expression of love given to someone else.

From then on it was our rewarding task to teach her to love and notice others and their needs. Even then the expression of her affection depended entirely upon her own particular mood and impulse. It was an immature and general thing. Only when she needed reassurance herself would she think of others, and say, "I love you, Daddy. Do you love me?"

It was not until she was four and became obsessed with counting and numbers that she began to express her love in a concrete way. She would rush in and offer to help with some troublesome task and say, "Mommy, I love you twenty-three." As she learned to count higher she raised her value number on her love as well, to express as much as her mind could comprehend.

She began to realize that words and deeds had to match, that a little girl who loved her mother "thirty-seven" did not leave blocks in the middle of the floor for her to pick up. She could not say, "I love you," with her lips and leave her tricycle in the driveway for Daddy to move when he was in a hurry to keep an appointment. Playmates did not listen to a little girl who said she loved, yet refused to share.

Slowly, the lesson began to take root in her impressive mind and heart: Love acts! Love gives! Love cares! Love is alert to the needs of others.

I am still working on this. It's so easy to forget that *talk* just won't get it; but love in action will. If I talk to others about the redeeming love of God, I must be Exhibit Number One of that love. What a tall order!

James wrote a whole book on the subject. His point was this:

"A man is justified before God by what he does as well as by what he believes. . . . Yes, Faith without action is as dead as a body without a soul."

(James 2:24, 26; Phillips)

A Time
To Laugh

It had been a happy day, climaxed by a fun evening, especially for a little three-year-old girl who had managed to cajole her daddy into chasing her around the house playing hide-and-seek and then to crawl under the big dining room table with a blanket an "play tent." Now it was bedtime, a bounce-up-and-down, giggly bedtime. I finally managed to stuff two wiggly legs and two flying arms into a pair of pajamas and to complete the regular routine, including reading from a favorite bedtime book, JOKES FOR CHILDREN. When it was time to pray, the giggling was only muffled. When her prayer was finished, I began an adult-type lecture on reverence. Her tiny voice, very serious now, finally interrupted, "Why, Mother? Doesn't God allow laughing?"

I stopped to reconsider. This had not been a case of disrespect at all — this was an earnest child sharing a happy time with Someone whom she had come to consider a personal friend. Of course, God allows laughing! But more than that, He wants His children to establish such a close relationship with Him that He becomes a natural partner in all the experiences of life.

There had been other nights, I remembered, when there was sickness or sadness and these too had been brought to God in simple, ardent prayer. God had shared the tears and the heartaches. Why not now the laughter? As I looked into those questing eyes, waiting for my answer, I was reminded of some very ancient and wise words:

28

"To everything there is a season, and a time for every purpose under the heaven:

A time to weep and a time to laugh; a time to mourn and a time to dance;

He hath made everything beautiful in his time...."

If God is the author of all the beautiful things, that includes those precious, happy times. Let's not hesitate to share them with Him!

Dear God,
Do You Remember...?

As soon as I picked up the receiver, my second pair of ears heard her feet pattering quickly up the stairs and across the upstairs floor. On and on the conversation ran, and back and forth the busy little feet pattered.

My mind went in three directions: listening politely to the caller, trying to think of a tactful and convenient time to excuse myself, and trying to imagine what was going on above. I was a frenzied wreck by the time I was finally able to say, "Goodby" in what I hoped was my regular Monday morning voice and hurry up the stairs.

A soft fragrance reached me as I stood on the landing, and I knew what I would find — the whole upstairs was blanketed under a fog of baby powder! I found her in a closet, her daddy's cap on her head, his huge shoes propped up on her tiny feet, and an incriminatingly empty powder can by her side. I grabbed up the little offender and planted her firmly on a chair to watch and "think about it", while I proceeded to sweep, dust, and mop the sticky, soft, shifting stuff, all the while lecturing (mostly to relieve my own tensions that had been building at the phone) about the virtues of doing right even when Mother's eyes are not watching.

When I had finished my long speech and the mopping, I hauled her out of the chair and down the stairs to collapse for a moment on the sofa.

She began to play so cheerfully that I was convinced she had forgotten the whole thing for she'd started to sing. It wasn't long, however, before she turned two very knowing blue eyes directly on me and sang, "Oh, be careful little mommy what you do. . . . There's a Father up above looking down in gentle love, so be careful little mommy what you do!"

Nothing more was said, or needed to be.

She was her cheerful little self all day. Night came and with it bedtime. Kneeling beside her bed she prayed softly, "Dear God, do you remember that powder . . . ?"

O Lord, another day has ended and here I am in your presence. . . . Do you remember that careless word, the less-than-Christlike attitude, the inconsistent moment? Do you have the patience to forgive me once again, and give me the maturity that will make me bigger and stronger and purer?
— Amen.

31

Kids Tell It
Like It Is

My husband and I, both college graduates, are writers of gospel music, an idiom of expression that is often considered illegitimate in the more sophisticated circles of high church music.

We have several friends in the music department of our local college with whom we often engage in philosophical discussions in defense of our choice of musical forms of expression. We have prided ourselves on being well-balanced, having chosen this form because it "speaks to the people." But at home, we truly enjoy gospel and country music best.

Recently, we were invited by a friend who is professor of vocal music to the large campus church to hear a concert performed by the college choirs and the civic orchestra. The church was full when we arrived so we were ushered to the front of the huge auditorium and seated among several of the college professors and their families.

Our three-year-old daughter sat quietly enjoying the concert until the orchestra began to play a quite spirited number, at which time she turned to the professor's wife and, pointing to the cellist, said aloud, "Well, will you look at that lady pickin' that orange guitar!"

O Lord, deliver me from the evil of falseness and pretense. Keep my sense of values straight; help me to never forget for one moment that the only status that matters is my soul's status in your sight. Help me to be like You . . . and then to be myself.

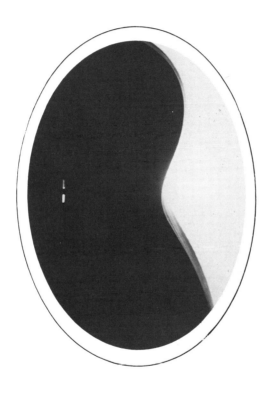

Look...
No Hands

The Statue of Liberty — such a familiar sight to Americans that most of us take its meaning for granted. We have seen this symbol of freedom and justice so often on travel folders and in advertisements that we hardly feel anything about it at all. But for a child, the gracious lady and her promise of freedom to all men everywhere is a new and profound experience.

It was with wide eyes that our little child first thrilled to this story. Often after hearing it she would bring a picture of the statue to me and ask some new question or beg me to repeat the inscription, and explain its meaning over again.

One day while watching a travel program on television, she saw a statue of the famous Venus De Milo. Without waiting to hear the narration, she ran to the kitchen where I was working and with terror in her eyes, she asked in a quivering little voice, "Mother, is Liberty dead?"

After I had explained about the statue of mistaken identity, and she had gone happily back to the program, the question she had asked lingered to haunt me. Dead . . . "Is Liberty dead?" Without arms — is it dead? If Liberty has no arms, is it dead?

Something has happened to our torch-fire of liberty. The cancer of impersonalization has eaten away at our culture until individuals have become faceless members of the mass. There has been a slow erosion from within of the respect for others. "Freedom" has undergone reverse evolution back to the barbaric struggle to preserve oneself with no regard for the needs of others.

Freedom has become distorted to mean the right of man to thrust a greedy fist into the grab-bag of our culture and take whatever and as much as he can make off with. Now, nearly too late, a few are beginning to awaken to the tragedy of our loss and are beginning to wonder what has happened to our true liberty and the awe-inspiring love of it.

From the lips of a child comes the shocking answer: freedom is not an inexhaustible resource that we can draw from forever with no thought of replenishing the supply. We do not possess an artesian well of liberty bubbling forth to quench man's thirst simply because we stand on American soil.

This freedom which we and our fathers have enjoyed has been bought with blood and sacrifice, paid for on the installment plan with each generation making its costly payment to preserve it.

Freedom is not a lollypop bestowed upon us by the benevolent past, but a burning, heavy torch. It must be shielded from the winds that would blow it out. It must be carried and lifted high by strong arms. Without arms, our arms, liberty is indeed dead! Does it have arms at your house?

"Give Me You"

She never said, "take me" or "carry me". From the time she could talk and toddle she would lift her little arms to me when she was weary, and lisp, "Mommy, give me you."

I never quite got used to hearing her say it, and each time she did, something stirred deep within my heart. She was asking for more than clean clothes, wholesome food, warm baths, an attractive house. She was asking for even more than nursery rhymes taught, stories read, questions answered. She said it not only with her upraised arms, but with her eyes and her mind and her soul: "Mommy, give me you."

Oh God, she's asking for *"me."* She is asking surely for comfort and care, but also something primitive — flesh calling out to flesh, blood to blood — something deep and eternal, a bond given us by God long centuries past that still calls together the souls of us. But she also wants to feel my uniqueness, my differentness from all other "mommies". There's something about the way things make me glad or mad or thoughtful that she wants to *know*. She wants me to share the tapestry of life as I see it. Then she can play her reactions off against that and come up with her own "me". Maybe that is what she's really saying — "Oh, Mommy, give me you, so in the years to come I can find myself."

So help me, Lord, not to be so busy cooking and dusting, scrubbing bath tubs and making beds, that there isn't time or energy left for me to give myself. Nothing else I give will matter if I cannot give her me and You.

"But We Don't Have a Happy TV!"

It was a sad movie and her sensitive little spirit always reacted deeply to whatever current of emotion happened to surround her.

The little boy in the story had to do without his Daddy most of the time because he was so busy with his business that took him out of the home on long trips. The mother was always struggling with the conflict between her own emptiness and that of being alone, and her desire to be cheerful for her little boy.

Suzanne's little chin quivered and she was close to tears as the story unfolded. "Mommy, please turn it off," she begged, but since the others present were engrossed in the play I explained to her that they wanted to watch the program and suggested that she should play with her puzzles or read a book in the next room. But the sad music and the mood of the story still reached her, and again she asked that the program be turned off.

I sat down at her little table with her and began to explain that there are families in the world who are unhappy, that there are little children in the world who do not have the kind of daddy that she has, that not all homes were like our home, and every house did not ring with love and laughter.

As she listened big tears welled up in her eyes. Finally, she burst out, "We have a happy home but, Mommy, we don't have a happy TV!"

The world in which we live is filled with tragedy and heartache. If we care at all we find ourselves very much involved in the sticky problems we would rather avoid.

Riots happen on our block. A young couple lose their baby and come to our home for strength and some concrete answers to their "why's."

An elderly lady is lonely and discouraged; we must tackle the sometimes tiresome task of telling her that she is needed, and then making her know we mean it by really needing her.

The "homebody" in me covets just one quiet evening with Bill and the children — a time to tumble and play, to read stories and sing, to sit on the porch in the dark holding hands while we listen to the soft and friendly night noises. But someone with a need comes by "for a few minutes", and our smaller needs must be set aside.

A seemingly innocent fifteen-year-old girl, an old friend of the family, casually drops in one morning and ends up sobbing out the fact that she is pregnant and wants to know how she can face life now, and her parents.

Nitty-gritty little realities. Life is full of them. Jesus invited those who dare to share His yoke and His cross and His cup. With all the courage we can muster, there are times when the plot just gets too thick and we would like to scream, "Please! God, turn it off, at least for a while!" But there are no OFF buttons to life, and we cannot just sit and watch. *We are involved* — whether we like it or not!

O Lord, you have made me care; now give me the grit to match my concern. Give me the courage to plunge into life's ocean of troubled souls with the buoy of redemption. Strengthen the earthly clay in me that would crumble under pressure and renew it with the steel of your strength and the resiliency of your love.

When the mortal in me would be weary in well-doing, help me to look forward to the beautiful harvest. Let me not just get involved, but to make a difference!

When I
Was Seven

It was one of those magnetic spring mornings. I slammed the screen-door back and bounded out through the tall grass as if drawn by some gentle invisible hand. I sprawled in the dew-dampened grass near the hedge and began to chew on the sweet end of a piece of long grass. I looked up into the incredibly blue sky. All around me was life! Even the fragrant breeze seemed to throb with its vibrancy. Suddenly, I was so overwhelmed with life that I felt that I would burst. How I loved the world — every grain and blade of it.

As I inhaled the beauty, I saw on the underside of a leaf a huge cocoon with dew glistening on the silken threads that encased the little life. The leaf shivered and suddenly the diamond-studded silk seemed an ugly prison to me. The love I felt for the whole earth turned to pity for the struggling creature inside.

There was a tiny hole in one end of the cocoon, and I could see the little life inside wrestle until it was exhausted, rest, then wrestle again. "I must help him," I thought. And with a heart full of childish philanthropy I pulled the leaf from the hedge. Bit by bit, tearing the tough silken threads back, I opened the cage. The warm sun and the cool breeze struck the wet little creature. To my surprise he did not stretch his wings and fly away; instead he only gave a feeble shudder and lay dead in my hand.

The days that have passed since that day by the hedge have clouded the lesson I learned. Like an infant I have had to be taught again and again that "our strength is made perfect in weakness."

How often have I thought that the cruel threads of life were hampering my progress and have prayed that God would deliver me from my problems, forgetting that the very "bonds" with which I struggled were making me strong and giving me the spiritual vitality I needed! Many times I would have shivered and died in my weakness had not God in his wisdom refused my petition!

Paul had this lesson to learn, for he, too, asked God to deliver him from some earthly infirmities. To this request God replied, "My grace is sufficient for you: for my strength is made perfect in weakness." And Paul said, "I glory in tribulation." Praise God for the tears!

Too often we give thanks for the sunshine of God's love, forgetting the gift of darkness when we must draw very near to see Light. It is easy to praise the Lord for "peace that passes all understanding," but what of the disturbing presence of the Holy Spirit that prods us when we become complacent? We bask in the joy of the Christian way, but how glad we should be, too, for the tears that bring us to our knees, for the burden of compassion that keeps us hungry to see those who have been forfeited as debris to the world, reclaimed and redeemed by the blood of Christ.

Yes, I am thankful for the times of spiritual exercise, for the dark days; because the greatest steps we take, even perhaps the very steps to our

conversion, are the result of one of God's greatest
gifts: the gift of tears.

Through my tears I met the Saviour:
    Through my tears I met the Lord.
Through my tears I see heaven's gates unfolding
    To the land where there shall be no more tears!

"Give Me The Works"

We could not be late. There was only a short time between the time Bill's meeting adjourned and flight time. Suzanne and I were to meet him right on time and drive him to the airport. There were no later planes; he had to be on time. It was this one or none. We pulled into the lot at the airport, ran to the terminal, checked the baggage, and noted the gate number of the flight.

"What time is it, Honey?" Bill called over his shoulder as he hurried up the corridor with Suzanne pattering close behind. I looked at my watch. "Well?" he said, impatient for my answer. But I could not tell him.

The silver watch band sparkled there on my arm, the crystal was clear and intact, the frame that held it was secure — but the watch, the works, the part that really mattered was gone. How I had lost it I did not know. Where or when it had dropped out I could not say. All I knew was that when I needed it most, it was gone.

I keep that watch band and the empty case and even wear it sometimes. No one has ever stopped me to tell me the "works" are gone. It looks very nearly perfect; you could hardly tell if you saw me on the street that it is only an empty shell of a watch. But it makes no sound, there is no movement, and the time it cannot tell. Actually, there is nothing there of any value at all. I keep it, though, to remind me. . . .

I may do all the right things; I may appear at all the right functions of the church. I may wear the proper clothes and the accepted hair-do and the appropriate facial expression. The facade may be very holy. But it is that which is inside that counts. If the "works" are missing, no one may notice it. Probably no one will stop me and say, "Pardon me, but I believe you have lost something!"

The loss may be so subtle, so gradual, and so silent that I may not even realize it myself. I could be too busy going through the motion of being a Christian to sense the loss.

It is only in times of stress, when the pressure is on, that I would discover to my utter amazement that the works were missing and I had been so busy doing and acting that I had forgotten the "being." It is possible to lose the real richness, the precious pearl of great price, the 21 jewel works somewhere along the way and not even know where, or when, or how.

So sometimes I wear that workless watch to remind me that the value is in the "being", and that is a daily thing.

Something Beautiful

Suzanne meant to make something beautiful. She had all the right materials: a fine sheet of construction paper, new paints and brushes, scissors and glue. And it started out all right. But right in the middle of the page when she was about half through, she dropped a big glob of paint by mistake. She tried to wipe it up, which only made the glob bigger. Then she tried to paint over it. That didn't work either. Then she tried rubbing it out, but that made a hole in the paper and on it went. It wasn't long before she was in tears. "Mommy, I tried to make you something beautiful, and just look! After that first mistake it just kept getting worse. Now it's just a mess and I can't fix it!" Her words managed to get through her disappointed sobs. I put my arms around her and tried to tell her that I loved her anyway. Then I remembered the extra sheet of paper I had up on the shelf. Now she could start again. Delighted with a new chance, she skipped away to begin anew.

Now about you. Remember the hopes and plans you had at first? Remember how you were going to make a success of your life, be something special? Remember those first little mistakes and how you tried to make the best of it all? But things just didn't seem to work out the way you thought they would and with one thing and another, before you knew it there just didn't seem to be any way out. No way. No way to patch and fix anymore. No way to cover it over. Then you woke one morning to realize that time was somehow slipping by, and you weren't getting any closer to those dreams and hopes you had — and all the time, life was speeding by.

Isn't it about time you just took the whole mess to the Heavenly Father and said, "Here it is Lord. It isn't what I wanted it to be. I had hoped to make something beautiful of my life but somehow it has turned out all wrong." Listen to me. God loves you. He's just been waiting for you to ask. He has a whole new sheet, a fresh start, a clean slate with your name on it. Wouldn't you like to just begin all over again?

PART II

"SAINTS"

Let's Talk
About Saints

This is about saints. Not porcelain, china, or gold-plated saints, but blood-and-bone saints. . . . Saints that plow fields and can tomatoes and nurse sick children . . . saints that clerk in dime stores, run punch presses and make dyes. From my earliest memories to this very moment, my life has been punctuated by precious moments with saints. They knew God. They shared the riches they had found and I was fortunate enough to be a bystander when these great lives were passing by.

They witnessed and testified, these saints, with great words and powerful prayers, but with other things too — things like pockets full of pink wintergreen mints that said to a child, "I love you . . . God loves you," and hot fresh bread and lemon pies and fried chicken from a warm kitchen — warm from cooking, warm from giving. Some had special ways of finding opportunity to share their story like picking up hitchhikers, giving haircuts, sewing little dresses, giving permanents — all the while, caring and loving.

Saints are not made in a day. Precious, sweet old saints get that way by being kind, thoughtful, concerned young people and involved, compassionate middleagers. I want to be a saint like some I've known.

Minnie
Hill

What I remembered most about her were her lemon pies and fried chicken, her grape arbor heavy with its purple harvest and the player piano, the pedals of which I could scarcely reach. And her hands . . . hands that loved the earth like she loved people, hands cracked into little rivers as only years of tender digging in the soil can do. Her flowers and her fruit trees, her grape vines and tomato plants responded to those hands much like the children in her class responded to her love.

She wasn't the world's greatest teacher, professionally speaking, but what she lacked in method she abundantly made up for in tender concern. She said so much by living that even a musty basement classroom, chalkdust and old Sunday school papers were powerless to muffle her message.

"God loves you. He has put you here for a reason, and life's only purpose is to find that reason and fulfill it." We heard. And most were obliged to do something about it.

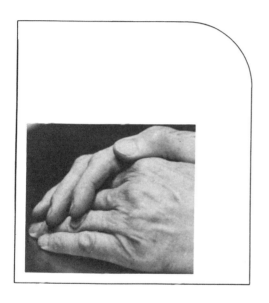

A Letter
from Home

Dear Gloria, Bill, and children,

It is good to be alive and see the fast-moving panorama of history being made in our world. We are living in explosive and important days.

But —

We are full of self-praise of our unheard-of achievements, and lazy with our luxurious conveniences. We have paid a dear price for progress, and have been robbed in the process of sacred beauties, smells, and sounds that only the wind in the pines can suggest. The tantalizing memories of common things are drowned out by the metallic clicking of great computers and the static interference of electric fences. Our speed and worldwide communications are marred by smog and antennas which pollute our air and mark up our skylines.

We strive to take a walk around the earth in endless space, and miss the joy of a simple walk around our gardens with a small child, the real wonder of the universe!

Yes, we accept these marvels with gratitude, but I am glad I have lived to see some other things, to *feel* the down-to-earth blessings of little pleasures, to hear the sounds of different springs and to smell the aromas associated with a much less complex life.

I am glad I have lived to remember:

A man plowing with a walking plow and a team of horses, his lines tied around his waist, and his dog following quietly behind him. I have smelled the fresh-turned sod, and watched silver winged blackbirds picking up fat worms in the last furrow.

A dash-churn, a wooden spoon worn thin from many stirrings, and bumpy from the tooth marks of little babies who have cut their teeth on its rugged edges.

A hand-hewn potato masher, and a "butter-print."

Fox-fire in a damp, dark woods, its eerie glow piercing the mist of a mucky swamp.

A one-room school house, with "dinner buckets" which were originally syrup-pails, standing in their shiny rows.

A "bobwhite's" nest, and turtle eggs hatching in the hot sand.

A mother opossum resting herself in the sun with her rat-tailed youngsters hissing, and tumbling over each other across her pouched belly.

An old-fashioned hog butchering, with barrels of scalding water, and kettles of rendering lard and sizzling cracklings. The after-treat of fresh country sausage and hot biscuits.

Sliced apples, and cut-off corn drying on snow-white sheets and covered with cheesecloth on the sunny side of a shed roof.

A dish pan full of wilted lettuce fresh from a spring garden.

A new-born calf getting a "wave-set" from his mother's wet tongue.

Lilies-of-the-valley bowing gently in the soft breezes around the tombstones in a country church yard.

A mother hen warning her foolish brood that a hawk is lingering near.

Trillium and May-apples blooming in a budded woods.

My father splitting logs along the river bank. I can still hear the quick out-let of his breath as the heavy mall made contact with the battered wedges.

Frozen ruts in a country lane, and ice designs in hoof-print puddles.

Mud dropping like too-stiff frosting from wagon wheels, throwing ruffled chunks along the road-way.

Real burning candles on a Christmas tree!

Home-made bread cooling on the reservoir of the old black, wood burning cook stove.

Hunting a bee tree, and stealing the honey.

The haunting call of the whip-poor-will at dusk.

Yes, it is interesting to watch on television the very battles of our men in the armed services on the other side of the world. It is marvelous to ride 80 miles an hour in the luxury of air-conditioned cars on our super highways. It is great to listen to stereophonic music, to enjoy push-button heating and have instant food . . . but there is a price to pay, and we are paying it.

Once, our big boys quit school to help "Dad." Now, we have shifty-eyed, shaggy-haired delinquents who roam our streets and shuffle down our halls in search of "kicks."

It seems that the more we obtain of this world's goods the less we really appreciate those who provide them. The more God gives us, the less we obey Him. I am sure this need not be, and Evil brings its own destruction. None-the-less, we are paying a price for progress, and I am glad I have known these other things.

Lovingly,

Mother

Mom
Hartwell

Mom was a little whitehaired Irish lady with big brown eyes and gentle hands. She reared eight children, lost two or three others to childhood diseases and had weathered many storms of heartache and tragedy. She and Pop had never had much, but what they had always seemed to be more than enough. Many had been the time when their tiny home had been mortgaged to keep the doors open to the little white frame church down the road. More than a few times children who had no place to go when tragedy took a parent, had permanently nested with the Hartwell brood. I never remember going to see them without leaving with something — a warm loaf of homemade bread, a dozen big soft molasses cookies or a cabbage from Pop's garden. Sometimes the things Mom sent home with us, we could not carry in a brown paper sack or in our hands — treasures so rich and fine they could only be held in our hearts.

It was one day soon after our first baby girl was born that we went out to Mom's house a little discouraged and tired from the pressures of our busy schedule. There never was a calf or pup, a kitten or a child that Mom didn't love and Suzanne was no exception. As I walked in the door that day Mom held out her arms for the baby. After she'd loved her and talked to her as only Mom could talk to a newborn, she gave her back to me and took an old battered hymnal from the piano bench. "Billy," she said, "our church bought new songbooks, so I brought this one home. Play through some of the old songs. Here is my favorite." As I rocked our baby and Bill began to play, Mom's alto voice sang what was the song of her life . . .

"I can see far down the mountain
Where I wandered weary years,
Often hindered on my journey
By the Ghosts of doubts and fears;
Broken vows and disappointments
Thickly sprinkled on the way,
But the spirit led unerring
To the land I hold today.

Tell me not of heavy crosses
Nor of burdens hard to bear,
For I've found this way so narrow
Makes each burden light appear;
And I love to follow Jesus,
Gladly counting all but loss,
Worldly pleasures all forsaken
For the glory of the Cross."

As I looked into the innocent face of our baby that day my heart bowed in prayer:

"Oh, God! May this moment and many like it be the heritage we bequeath this child. On down the road, when skeptics push her into some philosophical corner, may she point with certainty to folks like Mom and say, "I may not be able to define a saint, but there goes one."

The
Rugged Lady

She was a rugged lady — tall, fine, beautiful — but rugged. When but a girl herself she sewed together a muslin cover, lashed it to the wire bonework over a wagon and started across the country to homestead in Wyoming with her husband and two small babies. Years later I was to sit at her knee and listen to her tales of wolves, coyotes, heat and Indians. She told of lonely cowboys who would join the family for meals around the camp fire and spin yarns about their cattle drives.

There was not much sentiment or softness about her. Hers had been a difficult life in an untamed country and there was no time or place for frills. She was a master of all the arts of survival. She could create the latest fashion from a feed sack, make lye soap from hog fat, turn a hovel into a home. She could pull teeth, make soft curls or give hair cuts. She could dress a wound, bring down fevers; and once she bound a severed finger back into place, and by prayer and the sheer force of her will, made it grow back where it belonged. She hated dishonesty, weeds and grief. In her household there was never a floor left unscrubbed, a hole left unpatched or a wrong left unpunished. There was never a job that was too hard for her, or a demand on her that her energy couldn't match . . . Like the bleeding ulcer she nursed for 60 of her 80-some years — the only way we knew of it was the empty cream and Maalox bottles we sometimes saw in the trash.

The summer before she died she decided to put

a new ceiling in her bedroom. Rather than ask her children who lived 20 miles away for help she ordered heavy-duty plaster board from the lumber yard, sawed it into manageable squares, climbed a ladder and nailed them into place. She stripped the cracks, painted the finished ceiling and told us about it later.

I admired her and stood in awe of her but I never felt like she liked me very well. Now looking back I know that I misunderstood so much about her. As a child at special times, like Christmas and birthdays, I'd try so hard to find the gift that would finally win her approval. But no matter how hard I'd try, the response was always the same. She'd unwrap the gift, look at it, then put it carefully back in its box and put it away. She never wore or used the things I gave. She did seem to like getting money, so often my parents gave that. She had special places where no one was allowed to look. We did not go near her purse. Certain cupboards and closets that were full of locked boxes were irrevocably declared "off-limits" to prying eyes and inquisitive hands. It was only after she was gone, and then out of legal necessity, that we intruded with fear and trembling upon the privacy of her "holy of holies." What we expected to find I'll never know, but there in each box in their original envelopes were all the gifts of money all the children and grandchildren had ever given her. Sorted, totalled and bound by rubber bands, the bundles were labeled, "This is to bury me," "This is for the house payment," "This is for the fuel bill." And piled neatly in the boxes in which they'd been given, like hoarded jewels in a priceless collection, were all the gifts we had ever bought her. Going through the stack was like leafing back through the years, with the corresponding memories shifting out between the pages.

She had loved us all along. It was just that the crucible of the times in which she'd lived had forgéd a coat of armor around her, and the same shield that had protected us all from danger and hurts had also kept her from breaking out to tell us what she'd felt in her heart.

That last week, she'd mowed her lawn, weeded her garden, took a butcher knife and uprooted the dandelions in her yard so they wouldn't go to seed and spread the next spring. On Sunday she put on a roast and went to church. When the service was over she fixed dinner for Grandpa, washed the dishes, straightened the kitchen, took off her apron, folded it neatly on the foot of the day bed and lay down to rest. She died as she had lived: her soul and her house were in order and her work was done.

Dear
Julie:

It was so good to hear from you again. I think so often of the times we sat in the mud puddle at Grandma's house and made mud pies. Remember the time we mixed the mud with the "water" from that nice spigot on the barrel and chopped too-ripe cucumbers into our pies — then found out they smelled so strange because the "water" was kerosene? Remember the times we went berry picking in the woods out by the old abandoned car where the family of skunks lived and picked Grandma's big apron full of berries?

Remember the old coal-burning cook stove and the warm smell of homemade bread and the taste of fresh churned butter melted on it? Remember playing Flinch and Dominos and the smell of kerosene lamps, eating potato soup and listening to "Clyde Beaty's Circus," "The Green Hornet," "One Man's Family," and "Judy Canova"?

I can never forget Mom taking down the guitar (Remember how she played it, not like a guitar but like a harp?) and singing songs like:

> Blessed assurance Jesus is mine,
> Oh what a foretaste of Glory Divine . . .

When it was time for two little girls to go to sleep she'd put us in that tall, tall bed in that cold, cold room, then cover us with feather beds that seemed to get everything warm but our noses. And when she thought we were asleep I can never forget the sound of her kneeling on the linoleum at the rocking chair and the sound of her soft voice praying for us — that somehow God would guide our little lives and protect our souls from the traps of evil.

Julie, we are indeed rich! Such a heritage. They are fortunate who even meet a saint. We have walked with one — sat at her knee, touched her silver hair, felt the warmth of her abundant love. Oh, we weren't so special; she loved every child, every living thing. Her pink carnations and purple morning glories also felt her touch of tenderness. But we are rich because, as the highest of God's creation, He gave us the ability to love back, to return the affection. It is almost as great to be able to love back as it is to know you are loved.

Julie, I know you have gone through the doubts and confusion of life so common to the young who are struggling to know themselves, just as I have. But the longer I live the more convinced I become that real wisdom and real intelligence and true greatness belong to us only when we get big enough to become as a little child and believe in a Jesus who can make a difference in the way we live. When I compare the life — style and attitudes of a saint like Mom at the end of life to those of a person who has "hoed his own row" all his life, that is about all the proof I need. I don't believe in having a religion, but this thing of serving Jesus, betting everything you are and have on a way beyond proof really *works*.

Thank God for Moms like the one we've known

that say to us who would doubt, in lives more eloquent than words, *God is real!* Thank you for being a part of the precious memories of my childhood.

Even across the miles and the years I feel very close to you. Let me hear from you again — I wish the very best for you this year.

With love,

Gloria

Found in the Field

For the first time in months, Grandpa did not go with the trio to sing that first weekend in December. It was to be an over-night trip, so he stayed behind that Saturday to finish the plowing before the freeze. It was not two hours after the trio left that Grandpa was found in the field, fatally stricken with a heart attack.

The shock of his death was almost more than any of the family could take, since he had been in such good health, but far worse than the shock was the loss — and the emptiness that follows the loss — of a great little man. He was one of those rocks of humanity, a sort of "something-to-hold-to-when-all-else-fails" person, and we needed him.

That next evening the Oldhams came (at a time when a friend meant so much) and Bill was trying to tell them about this great life that had slipped from us. I was in the kitchen when I heard him, choked with emotion, say, "We loved him and we needed him much more, perhaps, than he needed us. We have no regrets, but if only he had not been found in the field . . ."

"Found in the field . . . found in the field . . ." The words stuck in my soul. This man died in the field. He lived in the field. He loved people — all people — more than anyone I know. He never saw crowd or a throng or a mob, he saw people: men and women and little children. And he loved them.

There were times when, to be honest, I wanted to get away from people. I wanted to retreat into my own little secure world. But not Grandpa. This *was* his world. He stayed in the field; he lived in the field.

Often when we were driving along he would say, "Look at that corn." I would look, and it would look like just a field of corn to me. But to him it was different. He saw the corn — the plants, the leaves, the roots, the soft young kernels. He knew if there was disease or blight; he knew if it was healthy and strong. That's the way he was with people. When I saw a group, he saw a lonely boy. When I saw a crowd, he saw the man who had worked for 37 years at the trailer factory and was worried about retiring. He saw them. And while I lived near the field, he was living in it.

Yes, he was found in the field. He would have been found in the field no matter where he died, for he knew Jesus and had heard him say something about a "field all white unto harvest . . ."

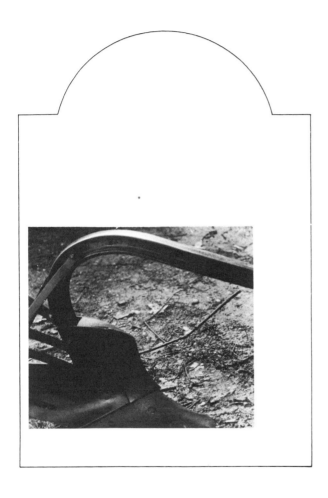

The Longer
I Serve Him

"Pop" Hartwell, Bill's grandfather, lay dying in the hospital; the death rattle was in his every breath. Bill was to bring Mom to be by his side, as she ever had been through more than half a century of sunrises and storms. They had known little of this world's goods, but they had known a love anchored in an exhaustless spirit of giving that had sweetened and grown richer with the years.

Leaning on Bill's arm, Mom left the old farmhouse and crossed the yard to the car. It was early July and glorious blossoms — the gems that adorn the crown of creation — dotted the landscape. I did not see them, for sadness and worry had blurred my vision, but Mom saw them. She looked up, her wrinkled old face brightening as does the sky when the first rays of sunshine peep through after the rain. "Thank God for flowers!" she said.

I glimpsed a revelation that day, for here in four simple words was the secret of unfathomless joy that runs silent, runs deep. A holy life had planted within her very soul an unshakable assurance that released her mind and made her able to see life's flowers at the darkest moment. Since we were a young couple still trying to bring into focus the true values of life, we were compelled even in this time of tragedy to ask this saint the question that would not be stilled in our hearts. "Mom," we dared to ask, "Does it pay to serve God — even now?" Though it seemed her world were crumbling around her, she looked straight at us through her tears. and with a surety and conviction such as I had never seen, she said, "The longer I serve Him, the sweeter He grows!"

At that moment, some misplaced pieces of life's puzzle fell into place for us.

"O Lord,
If You Had Been There!"

THEN SAID MARTHA UNTO JESUS, LORD, IF THOU HADST BEEN HERE, MY BROTHER HAD NOT DIED. BUT I KNOW THAT EVEN NOW, WHATSOEVER THOU WILT ASK OF GOD, HE WILL GIVE IT THEE.

An empty house where laughter once had
   rung . . .
A child's room, vacant except for one
   broken toy . . .
A brown bottle in a dusty corner, silent
   symbol of a ruthless tyrant . . .

O, Lord, if you had been there . . . !

Once-human voices bemoaning some
   "unpardonable sin" . . .
Sane facades miserably betrayed by
   insane eyes and hands . . .
The sterile corridors of a sterile hell . . .

O, Lord, if you had been there . . . !

The sickening brown and red of mud
   and blood . . .
Young thighs, twisted and bullet-ridden . . .
A conference table encircled with fat,
   unyielding faces . . .

O, Lord, if you had been there . . . !

A six-year-old scurrying into an alley with
   stolen loot . . .

A brick-strewn street lined with angry
   faces . . .
A weeping mother bending over a
   blue-uniformed corpse . . .

O, Lord, if you had been there . . . !

The silence of words never uttered . . .
The silence of no words to utter . . .
The silence that follows too many words,
   too quickly uttered . . .

O, Lord, if you had been there . . . !

   THEN JESUS SAID UNTO HER, I AM THE
RESURRECTION AND THE LIFE: HE THAT BE-
LIEVETH IN ME, THOUGH HE WERE DEAD, YET
SHALL HE LIVE!

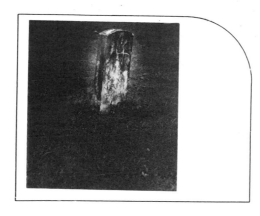

Mildred
Shaffer

Today, I got a letter from a teacher I had in the fifth grade. It was my birthday, and she never forgets things like that. She didn't remember me because I was special; in fact, I was just a regular, awkward, chubby kid who said silly things and made unnecessary noise. Other teachers would have considered me a waste of time and energy. I asked too many questions, climbed trees I couldn't get down from, and was a terrible tattle-tale. But to her, I was special. So were forty-eight other children in grades five through eight who made up our "big kids room," the upstairs part of our old two story frame school house.

Her working day was made up almost completely of overtime. I'm not talking about her hours (though on a typical day they ran from about 7:00 a.m. to 7:00 p.m.) but about the "beyond the call of duty" attitude with which she faced the day.

We went through the textbooks and learned the three R's all right, but there was much more: art projects, the materials for which she paid herself since there was no provision for such at our school, music and singing and rhythm band with Mrs. Shaffer at the piano. There were field trips and picnics, nature hunts and scouting. She was responsible for most of the lines of literature that I ever committed to memory. Long stanzas from the masters: Shakespeare, Plato, Longfellow, Whittier. Songs from our yellow *American Heritage* song book like "America The Beautiful," "Star

Spangled Banner," "Grandfathers' Clock," "Old Suzanna" and "Old Man River."

On Mondays we always answered the roll call with a quotation we'd memorized, and every morning began with the pledge of allegiance, prayer and the verses from the Bible we'd been assigned for that month. To this day I smell chalkdust and sweeping compound when I hear the 100th Psalm or the Lord's Prayer. We took turns going with her to special things at the little white Baptist church she attended. Sometimes she took us to her farm to feed the horses, and even to teachers' meetings and the evening classes she was perennially enrolled in.

There were some in the "upstairs room" who had never known anything like her gentle touch and soft words or the sight of her white head bowed in prayer over her brown paper sack-lunch. She was a rarity. For some she was the only contact they'd ever had with a real Christian. But she represented well the Lord she served and only eternity will reveal the countless lives she influenced.

Someday she will stand before the throne of God and shall hear words of praise from her righteous judge. I can almost hear her answer, "But, why? What did I ever do? I was just a teacher. I didn't even have a degree." Then I can see a parade begin to march by as once again the roll is read one final time, names that span the years — Tommy Jones, fifth grade, 1970; Marian

Stevens, seventh grade, 1952; Sally Morgan, sixth grade, 1961; Johnny Cane, eighth grade, 1956 . . . . on and on they march. And the Lord shall say, "Welcome home thou good and faithful servant. Thou hast been faithful in a few things. I shall make thee ruler over many. Enter into the joy of the Lord."

Uncle Jess

There are places Bill and I go and people we call when we need prayer and advice, good influence and a wholesome atmosphere — spiritual filling stations, I often call them . . . you know what I mean. There are times when we just give out until there doesn't seem to be any more to give and we come in from a weekend of ministering in a state of spiritual exhaustion.

At times like these we often call or visit Bill's great uncle Jess, who runs one of these spiritual filling stations. Jess knows how to pray; he has sort of a hot line to the Throne and being a spiritual nurse-maid for the tired and weary, the broken and bruised, is his special calling.

Nor are we the only ones who call on Jess. Bill's mother is a receptionist for a family doctor. Many have been the times when folks have called the doctor's office and instead of asking for the doctor have asked, "Mrs. Gaither, don't you have an uncle who prays?" She would mention Uncle Jess's name and the caller would say, "That's the man. Would you call him for me? We need him to come visit us and pray."

What a reputation to have! Better than any other sort of fame or glory — to be known as the town pray-er! I'd like to be a saint like that.